DE

FUNDAMENTIS . ASTROLOGIAE CERTIORIBUS

NOVA

DISSERTATIUNCULA AD COSMOTHEORIAM

SPECTANS

cum prognosi physica anni ineuntis a nato Christo 1602.

ad philosophos scripta

a

M. JOANNE KEPLERO,

Mathematico.

Vim coeli reserate viri: venit agnita ad usus:
Ignotae videas commoda nulla rei.
Sit labor in damno: faciet victoria lucrum:
Naturae ingenio vim reserate viri.

PRAGAE BOEMORUM.
Typis Schumanianis.

Thesis 1

It is generally considered the duty of mathematicians to write annual Prognostics. Since, therefore, I have resolved to afford satisfaction for the approaching year 1602 from the birth of Christ our Savior in limiting the prognostics not so much to the curiosity of the public as to the duty of a philosopher, I will begin rather with that which can be predicted most safely; a rich crop of prognostics for this year is forthcoming, as the number of authors is increasing daily, owing to the growing curiosity of the people.

Thesis 2

In those booklets some things will be said which time will prove, but many things will be refuted by time and experience as vain and worthless: as is customary with the people, the latter will be committed to the winds, and the former, entirely to memory.

Thesis 3

For truly, as the cause, so is the effect. In their predictions the astrologers, surrendering their pens to enthusiasm, carried away by it, admit causes that are partly physical and partly political, and for the greater part not sufficient, often imaginary, vain and false and partly, at least, of no value whatsoever. If they at times do tell the truth, it ought to be attributed to luck, yet more frequently and commonly it is thought that this comes from some higher and occult instinct.

Thesis 4

Some physical causes are recognized by all; others, by only very few people; indeed, many things exist naturally, but from causes hitherto known to no man. And of the causes which we know, there are some whose kind and nature we all usually understand, and others whose kind or indirect cause are understood by very few people, or by nobody.

Thesis 5

The most general, effective and certain cause that is known to all men is the approach and recess of the Sun. Now, the latter brings about the winter solstice, i. e. on December 21st, shortly before the sixth [hour] p. m.; and the summer solstice on June 21st at 10:30 p. m. [In the first case] then, there will be the cold of winter, whereas [in the second case], the heat of summer.

Note: Words in brackets were inserted by the translator.

Thesis 6

The nature of this cause can be seen from the following: At Prague, Bohemia, the altitude of the pole is 50° 5′ 45″. But the inclination of the ecliptic in this century is 23° 31′ 30″, as discovered by that Phoenix of the astronomers, Tycho Brahe, whom we have recently lost. Thus, the Sun, which is for us the originator of heat, does not shine for more than 7 hours and 49 scruples [minutes] above the horizon in winter, and thus heats our air for [only] a short time, and then lying [hidden] below the horizon doubly longer and more [completely] it ceases to heat. Yet, on the other hand, in the summer the sun remains for 16 whole hours and 22 scruples above the horizon and continues to heat, ceasing from this action only for a period less than half of that time.

Thesis 7

Yet air, as well as water and earth (as far as it is an element) except when continuously heated, returns at once to its nature [natural disposition], and grows cold. The [well-known statement] of Aristotle, that the nature of the air is hot *per se*, is false indeed.

Thesis 8

Whatever participates in matter, insofar as it participates in it, is cold by its nature. And whatever is hot by potency, has this nature from an animal force, either implanted or generated.

Thesis 9

Another and more important reason why the Sun, when it is high [in the sky], heats more than when it is low, is that when the Sun is low it strikes our horizon obliquely and weakly, whereas when it is high, it [strikes our horizon] more strongly at [nearly] a right angle. No one has been able to explain to this day why the immaterial solar ray behaves here in the same way as dense and material bodies when impinging upon each other.

Thesis 10

Therefore, as the Sun in summer passes almost four times higher than in winter at Prague, it follows from this and the above stated reason that on the shortest day there is not more than an eighth part of the amount of heat which descends to the elements [of nature] on the longest summer day.

Thesis 11

But not even all of this eighth part of the heat that is left in winter acts to our benefit. For the Sun, which rises but little above our horizon in winter, is set more obliquely against our thick air. Let us assume, then, that the surface of the vapid air, which refracts the solar ray, is at a perpendicular distance of one German mile from us (it could hardly be higher, for in fact, the altitude of the matter which produces the twilight, and of that which refracts the rays of the stars is not the same). Accordingly, a thickness of one and a ninth German miles is opposed to the solar ray in summer and three and a third [German miles] in winter. Thus, the solar ray is three times weaker in winter for this reason; and taking these three reasons together, in winter there remains barely a twenty-fourth part of the Sun's summer heat.

Thesis 12

Although these three causes are most evident on the very days of the winter and summer solstice, the cold will not necessarily be greatest on the former day nor the heat on the latter; there is in fact another cause, which of itself makes the winter more intense in the beginning of February and the summer in the beginning of August, or thereabouts. For earth and water are dense bodies, and cannot be heated instantly; when they are heated about the month of June, when the Sun is highest, they retain the deeply impressed heat for some time (even though they yield some limited amount of it towards the surface during the night), on account of the density of the matter and the magnitude of the bodies; therefore, they combine the heat of June with the heat of July and August. The same [holds true], conversely, with regard to the cold of winter.

Thesis 13

The same opinion should be held as to the second hour [2:00 p. m.] which is warmer than the twelfth, despite the fact that the Sun is already on the decline. In this case, the air shows the same behavior as the earth showed in the above stated case. For the air, being quite thin, certainly changes more quickly than the earth, yet not quite suddenly. And to this is added [the influence], if of not the whole body of the earth, at least of the surface.

Thesis 14

On the same basis one can predict that September and October will, for the same reason, be warmer than March and February, although in both instances the days will be of equal length.

Thesis 15

The moon presents another physical cause for predictions. It has been proved by experience that all things swell with moisture as the Moon waxes and subside as it wanes. This one thing

5

has been the cause of very many choices and predictions in economics, farming, medicine, and navigation. Physicists consider that the reason for this influence is not yet perfectly known.

Thesis 16

Yet the virtue of the Moon is two-fold: the first is the monthly one of which I have already spoken, depending on the mutability of the face of the Moon; the second .a semi-monthly one, and on that account even semi-diurnal,* which has the strongest power in medical crises and the reciprocal ebb and flow of the sea, [tides] which will be dealt with below.

Thesis 17

Therefore, on any day where a New Moon is found in the calendar, the moistures, as far as these depend on the Moon, will be decreased, whereas on the day of a full Moon, the moistures will be increased. But as in the cases just now mentioned, so also at the quarters, the moistures will be powerfully stirred. This is a simple and purely astrological prediction which, if it were deduced by the individual arts, the astrologer would have exceeded the limits of his profession, and he would have become agriculturist, physician, chemist, etc.

Thesis 18

Meanwhile, however, it is expedient that the same [limits] be stated. To the chemist, e. g., I offer this: it seems that the full Moon is adverse to the fusion of metals on account of the air being too moist. If this is so, there results a great choice of aspects for their work.

Thesis 19

The third physical cause for predictions is the varied nature of the remaining planets revealed by the colors themselves. Here we would err, if we would distribute the four usual qualities among the planets. For cold and dryness are not positive, but inherent and similar vital conditions of light, because cold and dryness are greatest where all light, all life, as well as all heat are absent. Thus, as nothing comes down to us from the sky but the light of the stars, the cold, assuredly, and the dryness do not come down *per se*.

Thesis 20

Our deduction of the various actions, number and strength of the planets is different from, but not at odds with, Aristotle's

---

*"Influences Solaires Lunaires sur le Naissance Humaine," by K. E. Kraft, results of an investigation of astrology (1923-1928)—see June, 1941, issue of American Astrology Magazine, page 38.

[method of deducing] his four elements from the four qualities. All variation is due to contrariety, the first variation being due to the first contrariety [and so on]. In his Metaphysics, Aristotle, wishing to philosophize on a higher and more general level than geometry, accepted as the first contrariety that which exists between *same* and *other*. To me it seems that diversity in things is created from nowhere other than matter, or from occasions caused by matter, and where there is matter there is geometry. Thus, what Aristotle called the first contrariety is without any middle [element] between *same* and *other* and I find philosophically considered geometrics to be the first contrariety indeed, but with a middle [element], and in such a way that while *other* was to Aristotle one term, we break it up into *more* or *less*, i. e., two terms. Now, since geometry has offered an example to the creation of the whole world, this geometrical contrariety is not improperly concurring in the decoration of the world which consists in the diverse forces of the planets.

Thesis 21

But as these terms—same, other, equal, more, less—do not denote anything *per se,* one must think of the subjects themselves. Now, the subjects or natural things with which these expressions deal are derived from this. The most wise Creator proposed to Himself to create a corporeal world. As soon as He conceived man, He conceived matter, which we know, according to Moses, to have been water, which is wet, tractible, yielding. Moisture then, is one natural matter. Yet the body of the world did not satisfy the Creator, unless it became similar in a certain measure to the Creator, by assuming life and motion. This, then, is the second thing, that is to say, life. Now, since we are dealing with the powers which the stars exercise upon the people of this lower world, we ought to consider what really comes down to us from the stars. This certainly is not the matter or body itself, because this was present before. Nor is it life itself, originally, for this is derived by all living creatures from a stirring of the vital principle that exists within themselves. This means the stars do not create, but do render assistance. Consequently, they are performing the function of an instrument. Therefore, they impart to us qualities of an instrumental character, namely two—according to the number of two natural things, to wit:—(1) moistening power in order to render matter manageable; (2) heating power to support life and motion. They obtain and exercise both qualities through the benefit of light, which send down to us continuously. Thus, the proper quality of light, so far as it is direct light, is

7

heating; whereas the quality of light, so far as it is reflected, is moistening.*

Thesis 22

Therefore, we have two faculties: heating and moistening, in a three-fold variation, if you will: excess, moderation and deficiency. Let us see how many varieties follow therefrom. First, there may be solitary faculties: heat, in excess, in moderation, or insufficiency; and moisture, in excess, in moderation, or insufficiency. This makes six varieties. Then, from the combination of both faculties there originate nine varieties as seen from the Table given herewith.

Hence there are fifteen varieties in the universe. Now let us see what is the choice among them and which are naturally to be rejected.

Thesis 23

First the existence of any solitary excess or deficiency without compensation, is not possible. Hence, of the six solitary faculties, four are eliminated. There is the moderation of heat (we will consider the moderation in proportion to the world, and not by the quantity) that resides in the Solar body and uses merely its own light; [there is] the moderation of moisture which resides in the Lunar body and uses merely the borrowed light of the Sun and the stars.

Thesis 24

Next, neither an accumulation of an excess nor that of a deficiency could expediently develop. For excess and deficiency of heat and moisture are somewhat different by nature, and are obtained only when tempered by mixture. Thus, no planet gets both faculties, either the excess or deficiency. Consequently there remain but seven varieties out of the above mentioned combinations. Furthermore, there also fall away twice two out of these. For the ratio of the excess of heat to the moderation of humidity is the same as [the ratio] of the moderation of heat to the deficiency of moisture; and ratio of the deficiency of heat to the moderation of moisture is the same as the ratio of the moderation of heat to the excess of moisture, which could be represented by parallel lines in a lineal figure. The same opinion holds as to conjoint excesses or deficiencies. Consequently, there are five true varieties: three simple ones; and two double ones, as is al-

---

* In the book "Tertius Interveniens" Kepler retracts this opinion by stating: "Now it seems to me more proper that the moistening power is derived from the matter of the sphere."

ready clear, or rather two names and one variety of three names. And since there are also five planets in the world, three superior and two inferior, for this reason alone (although others are at hand) it certainly is proper that they have been created in such a number; nothing indeed could be more apt than this distribution of the combinations among themselves, which I wish to present by means of the following table:

```
                     I  V  P  I  T  E  R      Excessus
        /Excessus                                        \
                 S  mer               S  S
                    A      cu     V      R
                       T   N    ri   A
Sol.  {                VE    V    M     us              } Humectandi  Luna.
Calefaciendi  Mediocr. I  V  P  I  T  E  R      Mediocritas
                    mer    S    R    S
                       R   cu    V    N
                    A      N    ri     V
                 M  VE               us  S
        \Defectus    I  V  P  I  T  E  R      Defectus  /
```

Thesis 25

From this it follows that the five planets not only use borrowed solar light but also add something of their own, which in fact is suggested by other reasons. For if many of our physical bodies [on earth] have an innate light, what prevents the other heavenly globes besides the Sun, having the same light? Also if the planets were lacking their own light, it seems they should also change their face, like the Moon. It is highly credible that brightness and sparkling are evidences of light in itself, while nebulosity and dullness are evidences of foreign [or reflected] light.

Thesis 26

We should now also consider what enables us to distinguish these powers of the planets in relation to excess, moderation or insufficiency. As we have inferred [re] the borrowed light from reflection, various modes of reflection which result from various surfaces are to be considered for this variation. I refrain from speaking of the [particular] reflection which comes from the surface of a mirror and is reflected from any point to any other point; I speak rather of that reflection which we perceive on any wall, even on an uneven and rough surface, which reflects the light impinged thereon, imbued with the color which it possesses from any point thereof into the entire hemisphere. For the light of the Moon reflected to us comes in the latter, not in the former way; otherwise we would not see the horns in the Moon, but a

9

small ever-round image of the Sun. Therefore, the geometrical arrangement the surface produces is necessarily due to the spots [irregularities] we see on the Moon's surface.

Thesis 27

The causes, however, of some or other reflection (the cause of the quality in the reflected ray) are the colors of the reflecting surface. Here [at this place] I should like to hear from the chemists precisely what [it is that] causes the variation of the colors in the terrestrial bodies. To be sure, colors of the rainbow are divided into two classes: the first results from the darkening or absence of light, and the other from the refraction or coloring. The beginning of either class is from the very light, or a white glow analogous to light, which, occupying the middle circle of the rainbow, cuts it [the circle] as it were, in two. For indeed, on one side it is broken into pieces [split up] and on the other, refracted; and on either side [end] it dissolves into black or darkness. In the first band of the division it is golden yellow; in the second, red; then, dusky; and finally, black. The same appears in the clouds at either sunset or sunrise; the same in the stars near the horizon; the same at solar eclipses, when our eyes, in which there is this delusion, are suddenly deprived of the light of the Sun. In the first band of the reflection, however, is seen green; next, azure; then, purple; and finally, completely black or darkened. Since, therefore, this is the order of the colors of the rainbow, it is proper that the same [order] is also in the reflection; that a white surface reflects the ray in the strongest manner; then [second] a green and golden yellow [surface]; then an azure and red; then purple and dusk, while a black surface reflects it the least.

Thesis 28

Now a black surface when strongly illuminated, will emit a red ray. This is apparent from a steel mirror where the white color of the face and the black color of the mirror when confused present the face somewhat ruddy. This is the reason one would state quite correctly that the star Mars has a black surface, because its ray is very ruddy. Therefore, its reflected light is weakened; hence there is an insufficiency of moisture. By the same evidence of color and moisture, we will attribute to Saturn a white, rough [uneven] surface, because it is lead-colored; to Jupiter, a red or purple [surface] because it appears golden-yellow reddish; to Venus, a golden-yellow or white and most uniform [surface], as it is the most beautiful; to Mercury, a dark blue [azure] or green [surface], as it appears silver colored, [being] bright more on account of its sparkling or subdued shine than by its color.

Thesis 29

To be sure, the light itself is also varied by the surface of the body whence it comes, as it shows now this and that color, but the degree of the heating power is obtained from the interior disposition of its body. But even the surface itself indicates the disposition of the body, the moistening power being dependent on the heating power in a certain measure. And indeed, if color can be transferred and propagated from one body to another by the intervention of light, it is credible that other qualities also can be transferred; for as to the color this is most certain. Whence it appears to be proper that the disposition in the body of any planet itself will be analogous to the power shown in effect by the planet. And if this is admitted, it may lead us to wonderful theories. For instance, I would say that it is unwholesome to live in summer opposite a wall illuminated by the Sun because the quarried stone consists of lime which, as it has the power of corroding and consuming, also imbues with this property the ray that it reflects. Now, in the first place, it appears that some pellucidity pertains to its own light. For if a thing has its own light, it certainly is not lodged in the surface but is rooted within the depth, as we perceive in precious stones. Consequently, if a thing is transparent, it must be pellucid. To be sure, many things become transparent by heat itself, and this is retained in their disposition.

Thesis 30

The philosophers may excuse my drawing conclusions from the bodies we have on hand to the heavenly bodies. For they [the philosophers] themselves, certainly do not indicate any differences at all in those bodies. Wherefore let them admit with equanimity these base and terrestrial differences among the heavenly bodies. For it is preferable to say something which does not involve any palpable absurdity than to be silent altogether. And, indeed, I do not know whether one ought not to call divine and heavenly the quality in the gem carbuncle which furnishes that little light, rather than call divine the elementary heating quality of the Sun. Therefore, I state that Saturn exceeds in humidity, but is deficient in heat; that it is to be likened in the disposition of its body to ice (which is likewise very humid, since it is really water deprived of all heat), whence it has a white surface and therefore the internal disposition is denser and not quite transparent. The astrologers state that it is cold and dry, which is almost the same thing. Yet since Saturn makes the summer rainy and the winter

11

snowy, it deserves rather to be called humid. We attribute to the body of Jupiter a similarity to a ruby, as it is transparent on account of its own great light, also uniform, and red on account of its brightness and color. Mars will be compared to a glowing ember, from which the inside latent fire shines forth; for the astrologers assert, and it is proved by experience, that the power it brings about is torrid and fervid with heat. To Venus we will attribute electrum [an amber colored metal] of a uniform and golden-yellow surface, on account of its extraordinary and saffron-colored shine; so that it does more moistening than heating, which property seems to require a soft body. Lastly, Mercury will be likened to the sapphire or the like, in that it is impregnated with the clear acuteness of its rays, and that it admits more of its own than foreign light as it has that combination where the heat conquers moisture.

Thesis 31

As to the planets' humidity and the extent to which their light is borrowed, one may consider their emersions or occultations [eclipses] and oppositions. Saturn, being in opposition to the Sun on May 11th and conjoined to the same on Nov. 18th, at both positions will exercise in the highest degree the moistening power which it possesses, because it turns its full face, illuminated by the Sun, towards us. This moistening power will be least on February 11th and August 9th in either quartile [square]. Jupiter, similarly, will be in opposition (to the Sun) on April 8th, and on October 26th in conjunction; whereas similarly on January 8th and July 6th it will be in quartile. Mars, likewise (little moisture that it has), will be in opposition to the Sun on March 5th, whereas on June 9th it will be in quartile successively in the intervening and following periods of time. Venus has a different effect and so has Mercury. For on May 15th, conjoined to the Sun above, its moistening power is great before (the conjunction), later growing successively less; and in the following year, conjoined to the Sun below [it moistens] the least. Similarly, Mercury is scant [in moisture] on January 4th, April 30th, August 29th, and December 19th. For on being conjoined to the Sun below, it turns upward its whole face, illuminated by the Sun; but it [moistens] most of all on March 9th, June 27th, October 19th, when it conjoins the Sun above, and turns its lighted face down.*

Thesis 32

There is doubt as to the light and proper power of heating; whether the high [planets] or the low ones are stronger. The

* The words "above" and "below" as used here evidently refer to Celestial Latitude, i. e., "above" meaning the conjunction takes place when Venus is north of the ecliptic.

high ones seem more powerful to the astrologers, while the low ones are the choice of the physicists. We consider that a compromise is necessary here, that the greater the angle in which the low planets are seen, the more they heat, precisely because of being seen in such a manner. But the power increased by altitude has a different cause.

Thesis 33

As to the reason for both the power of heating and that of moistening, one should consider in what [zodiacal] sign the planets are situated. For both the planets and the moon operate at the maximum in Cancer, as they are then longest above the Earth because of the other reasons mentioned in the beginning when we were dealing with the Sun. So also they have more power when they are in the Northern part. Therefore, the winter full moons are more humid than the summer full moons. Thus, in the Northern zones for this year and the following few years the above explained powers of Saturn and Jupiter, nay, even Mars at the end of the year, will be weak because they will be situated in low [zodiacal] signs, but in the southern zones they will be, in the same measure, stronger.

Thesis 34

Since we see that whatever is slowest in motion can perform the most we deduce the reason why the stationary [planets] are so very effective when situated at their apogees. When Mercury stands still it is most effective of all the planets, for being the fastest it also loses the most speed. On the other hand, Saturn in a stationary position has the least effect, because it has little [speed] to lose in the standing still. And the stationary position of Mercury indeed causes wind, snow or rain, and generally copious vapors. Therefore, we shall expect these about January 17th, April 20th, May 12th, August 15th, September 6th, December 9th and 31st. But the motion of Mercury, still uncertain, does not allow the determination beforehand of the exact date.

Thesis 35

These causes of future events which I have explained so far, although they have, in fact, a great deal of divination, yet all portray their own nature more closely than that which will follow. For their way [mode] of acting consists in some outflow of light which continues to these sublunar bodies, which outflow, although it is without substance and is timeless, yet is not without limit of quantities. For it proceeds in a rectilinear course; it is lessened with [increased] distance from the start; it increases and decreases in conformity with the face itself of the lucent planet;

13

it is hindered by interposition of any opaque body; and on the other hand, it is supposed [to flow] continuously, assuming a star to be of considerable prominence. This applies not only to one and the same star, but also to the comparison of different [stars]; and since the Sun and the Moon are greatest in aspect, these powers are also most evident in them; in the other planets whose diameters appear small as compared with the diameters of the Sun and the Moon these powers are scarcely appreciable. Still, variations of these qualities in the manner indicated, are almost neglected even by most astrologers.

Thesis 36

Now there follows another cause which concerns equally all planets and is far better known and much more admired than the former. This (cause) does not encompass anything material, but has a kind of form, with a mental faculty, with understanding, with a sense of geometry. It does not obtain its strength from single stars in straight lines, but combines the rays of the two stars meeting on the earth, whether they meet geometrically or "alogically"; nor is it extinguished by the face of the silent moon itself when no rays descend to the earth, but the ray is then imagined as descending; it is not hindered when the Earth is placed between us and the stars, but is produces latent stars below, even real stars above. Lastly, it is almost instantaneous, and on changing its geometrical angle to an "alogic" and an "harmonic" one, it is at rest immediately or a little later, although the lights of the stars are increasing. As these have been very reliably confirmd by experience, the following opinion will suffice for me.

Thesis 37

As God the Creator borrowed the decoration of his corporeal world from a corporeal form which is quantity, it is proper that the places themselves, indeed, the spaces themselves and the masses themselves of the bodies, were picked out in such a mutual proportion as originated from regular kinds of solid figures, which I demonstrated in my Misterium Cosmographicum; while the [movements] of the bodies, which [constitute] the life of the world may either harmonize pleasantly or cooperate strongly in the case when they have a proportion chosen from ordinate [regular] planes. For as the plane is an image of the solid, so [also] is the motion an image of the body, and inasmuch as no more than five solids are possible in geometry, so also the harmonic relations originating from the comparison of the ordinate [regular] planes could not be more than eight, which I shall, please God, demonstrate at some other time in a book entitled Harmonics.

Thesis 38

Now, there are eight kinds of form-giving motions, and the action of the heaven upon the Earth is (as it were) effected through the stellar rays which meet on the Earth and form angles, hence the eight harmonic modes will depend upon the dimension of these angles. To be sure, the ancients did not, indeed, admit more than five (*aspects,* as they are generally called) : conjunction, opposition, square, trine, sextile. Yet my mind told me first to add three: quintile, biquintile, sesquiquartile, which have subsequently been confirmed by manifold experience.

Thesis 39

I can assert no other reason why the activity of double planets proves so effective at the exact focus of aspects than that of animate faculty, which on the one hand is capable of a geometric ratio (which forms the aspect) and on the other hand rules over the body in which the operation is observed. For this does not take place because the rays unite in one angle: some angle will be formed by two rays on both the day before and the day after the aspect, in fact, perpetually; but the activity occurs precisely when the angle has a harmonic ratio or scheme (in fact, Ptolemy called it schematism). Yet no efficiency attaches to the ratios or schema *per se.* In this case the same thing takes place as usually occurs in the locomotion of animals. It would be philosophizing absurdly to say that an animal can move the objects of sight entering through the eye and that the animal does not need for this purpose the faculty [capability of motion] in the moving body itself.

Thesis 40

Now this faculty which gives power to the aspects does not reside in the stars themselves. For these aspects of which we speak occur on the Earth and are a mere apparition which does not really proceed from the activity of the stars, but from an accidental position of two stars with respect to the Earth. Inasmuch then, as the vital force moving the bodies is not in the object, but is where a species of the object is represented [inherent to a whole species or idea, of objects], so this power which gives rise to efficient aspects, must of necessity be contained both in all sublunar bodies and in the huge terrestrial globe itself. That is to say, all animate faculty is an image of the "geometricizing" God in creation, and is roused to its action through this heavenly geometry or harmony of the aspects.

Thesis 41

To the inconsiderate person, the new form of Philosophy will seem to be what it is not, unless I generalize somewhat upon

15

the ancient dogmas hitherto prevailing. Firstly, as regards the Earth, no one will deny that the form of its whole, as far as it is a whole, is more perceptible than that which is discernible in any clod [of earth]. Truly its very works, which are the generation of metals, the preservation of terrestrial heat, the exudation of vapors for the progeneration of streams, rains and other atmospheric conditions, show that it arises from this kind of animate power. These prove that its form is not simply one that preserves, as in the case of stones, but altogether one that enlivens [quickens].

Thesis 42

Yet it is not necessary on that account that the Earth grow or be moved [from its] place. For its life is neither human nor properly animate, nor of any family, but is a peculiar species, whose definition has resulted from its activity, just as other species of animate faculties. And the [same] reason which prompted the ancients to assert the existence of a third species of life force in planets, prompts us to assert the existence of this fourth in the Earth.

Thesis 43

Nor would it be absurd for animate faculties which are not used in [articulate] reasoning, to be able to understand geometry, and to be moved by it as if by some object. There are examples which are easy to concede. The plastic [form-giving] faculty of a tree is not reasoning; and yet at the command of the Creator it carries out to the utmost the arrangement of the leaves for the benefit of the fruit and for a definite end. Nay, even all seeds retain the beauty that results from numbers. Very many kinds of plants have the quinary [leaves arranged by fives]; not by material necessity transformed from tree to apple, in which transformation the conservation of a quinarium would be impossible; but by the communication of the form-giving power which has the beauty innate to a quinary arrangement. But the above relation is more obscure and less wonderful, because the power remains in itself and propagates the quinary that it possesses. I will give a more suitable example. The rustic does not consider what geometric proportion a sound has to another sound. And yet that extraneous harmony of stringed instruments flows into the mind through the ears of the rustic and cheers the man. However, this is not accomplished by the moderation [regularity] of the mingling of sound, nor by the gentle soothing of the ears (for violent sounds are often hurtful to the ears and nevertheless their harmonies cause delight), nor by any other cause hitherto ascertainable, but on account of one thing, as I shall demonstrate in the Harmonics, because geometry provides the form of the harmony.

Therefore, elated by these examples as if elevated by some steps, let us venture to ascend even to the summit, in that we believe that there is an enlivening animate power in the Earth, and that in the animate power there is some sense of geometry, because this power is of the kind of animate faculty, which, although it always applies itself to its work, is stimulated in a higher degree when nourished, as it were, by harmonious aspects. In like manner, then, as the ear is stimulated through harmony to listen attentively and to hear so much more (seeking this enjoyment, which is the perfection of sensuous perception), so the Earth is stimulated by the geometrical union of the quickening rays (in fact, we stated that they heat and moisten) in such a way that it (the earth) applies itself so much more to the work of quickening, and exudes a great abundance of vapor.

Thesis 44

However, although these influences of the aspects do differ somewhat from the various natures of the planets themselves, explained above, the Earth is influenced by the geometrical mingling of the contrarities of Saturn and Mars in one way, while it is influenced in another way by the corresponding contrarities of Jupiter and Venus, almost in the same manner as we observe that in the bowels of man any purgents cause movements of liquids but rhubarb especially causes those of the bile; (for is not a geometry-capable faculty, capable also of color and of other qualities in the rays?); but the principal diversity comes from the disposition of the bodies, particularly of the Earth, which is different at different times in different places. When, in the spring time the moistures are plentiful in the middle of the Northern part of the Earth, owing to the approach of the Sun, of which we have spoken above, even the mildest aspect of any planet excites that power of the Earth so that it is stirred up and exudes a certain quantity of vapors for producing showers. At some other time or place the strongest aspect by far can stimulate the Earth indeed, yet it may elicit but little owing to the insufficiency of matter.

Thesis 45

At this juncture another cause should be understood which, moreover, has not been known heretofore; and the ignorance of this cause interferes very much with the predictions of the Astrologers. For as there are some periods of moistures in man which cause him to be frequently in some mood without any evident cause, sometimes he is merry, even without music, [yet] on the other hand [sometimes] he cannot be diverted from melancholy thoughts by any pleasant things; entirely similarly I see that in

17

addition to the aspects there exist other stronger and more lasting causes which bring about the result that some whole year, [even] during the periods lacking in aspects, has excessive moisture and hence also cold; in such a year you would see that even the mildest aspects, as often as they occur, produce the greatest number of rain or wind, as happened in this current year, 1601. Whereas there is so much dryness in some other year that on the days of the aspects only small clouds, or fumes are evaporated instead of vapors, as occurred in the year 1599.

Thesis 46

I refrain from considering whether this manifest diversity originates from the eclipses of the Sun and of the moon (which are equally to be included among the aspects, that is to say, among the conjunctions and oppositions). Thus, it should be held that the same animate faculty of the Earth, of which I have spoken so much, is strongly disturbed by the sudden loss of light, and is subjected to an affection which continues for a long time, which Theophrast,* who does not always tell fables, seems to have felt. For unless you choose either this cause, or reject all physical causes and assign this regular work of nature to an extraordinary providence of God, you will not be able to explain why eclipses are so portentous.

Thesis 47

Yet it is more proper that the same thing occur to the Earth as to animals, without regard to mortality, [namely] that the Earth has, by some internal disposition, its periods of moistures or something like diseases; if so, the laws and times of the periods should be investigated through a comparison of the observations of many years, an investigation which has not yet been done to this date. Caesius attributed here something to a nineteen year cycle of the moon, to which we cannot deny faith entirely. For it is claimed by the maritime people also that the greatest tides of the sea revert after 19 years on the same day of the year; and as the moon is destined to [govern] moistures, she may seem capable of such influences.

Thesis 48

A third cause also recommends itself by its great likelihood; many disturbances of sublunar nature, which I earlier declared to occur during an absence of aspects, are produced by harmonic motions of the planets. For truly, if the proportionate angle of the rays effect this, why not also the proportionate motions of

---

* Paracelus.

18

double stars as often as they strive for one and the same harmony, so that one pervades some equal space more quickly and another more slowly in harmonic proportion. For, in fact, these ratios are variable and do not often occur, for the same planet is sometimes faster, sometimes slower. But these have not yet been confirmed by experience, nor has any method yet been devised for the investigation of harmonies of this kind.

Thesis 49

The Astrologers seek the vainest cause for this general disposition of the year in the entry of the Sun into Aries, [the disposition of] the four seasons in the cardinal signs, and the months in the figures of lunations, as if TIME were some permanent subject like man, whose horoscope we could examine with reason, and not rather as a part of the celestial movements, or as if the Earth were revived at one moment for a new summer. The Earth is changed, indeed, by the aspects of the vernal figures, as far as there are any, not only on a [given] day, but on preceding and following days by other [aspects] and [again] others, which happen any [given] day.* But there is nothing more improper in this almost unique solicitude of some astrologers than [the fact] that by some puerile credulity, contrary to all sound and philosophical reason, they allot the twelve houses among the seven planets [and] claim dominations and momentary vicissitudes of empires as in like relationship of men, whence arises all magic and astrological superstition. Let us grant that at some place a [certain] likelihood is produced by this distribution, as in [the case of] Saturn, to which the signs of winter are attributed; but this is brought about by other causes, and again in other [cases], as when vanity is derived from Jupiter. This frivolous part of Astrology has been refuted (rejected) some time ago on physical grounds by the astrologer Stoefler** (without looking for evidence from [Pico] della Mirandola,† the enemy [of Astrology]); and it is daily refuted by experience, as during so many centuries hardly any definite time of an equinox was known to them, as has been shown by Tycho Brahe. Yet some [astrologers] adduce the [Sun's entry into] cardinal signs of past years, and compare them with the effects; I will in due time show that they were false and that the true figures, on examination by the same false

---

* Kepler evidently did not consider transiting aspects to planets in cyclic-horoscopes, equinoxes, solstices, lunations, as valid bases for judgment, but preferred to refer events to mutual transiting aspects as they occurred.

** Johann Stoefler (1452-1531), Professor of Mathematics & Astrology.

† Count Pico della Mirandola in his book entitled "Disputatio contra Astrologos," of which Kepler treats more in his book "De Stella Nova."

methods, proved to be contrary to the qualities [observed] in the following years. In the coming year (1602) the Sun enters Aries on the 20th of March by sunset, while Jupiter rises in Libra; the astrologers will consider that Gemini shall rise according to the Prutenic (Prussian) tables.* Yet no general significance may be deduced from this. For Jupiter reveals his powers on April 8th, when in opposition to the Sun, but on May 10th-11th [the influence of] Saturn succeeds that of Jupiter, because Saturn is opposed to the Sun on that day.

Thesis 50

Here however, I do not reject the [well known] observations of the ancient authors, Hesiod, Strates, Virgil, Plautus nor other modern [observations] of agriculturists, who draw conclusions as to the future temperature of the air from the annual rising of the stars and phase of the Moon at the time they observe these phenomena (not a long time beforehand). For they do not consider these observations as so many magic signs in the heavens, nor as the cause of a future constitution (for at different years they get a different omen), but as a sign of a general terrestrial disposition which is already present and is going to continue for a certain [period]. But regarding the laws governing these periods I have to admit my ignorance.

Thesis 51

Moreover, it has been noticed that this succession of universal qualities is characterized by short periods. Thus the rustics (who know this best), when they have observed a hot summer, expect a very severe winter. And if an unnatural warmth continues during some part of the winter they expect that the last part [of the winter] will be so much colder. Thus, at the time when a severe winter sets in very early, there will, in turn, be an early Spring in harmony with most of the aspects that occur during this time of the year.

Thesis 52

I have reviewed the principal grounds for astrological predictions; what is left I intend to exhaust to the utmost in the predictions themselves. Firstly, the months December, January and February will have the sextile of Saturn and Mars, which will be of exceedingly long duration. For if it happens that Mars is stationary during this time and Saturn is slow *per se,* [there will be] a violent disturbance and a most conspicuous excess in

---

* Translator's Note: Noting certain astronomical tables of Reinhold published in Prussia in the 16th Century.

20

the state of the air. But it is not so easy [to say] in which way there will be an excess. For this it would be necessary to make a general investigation of the disposition of the Earth, which will prevail, and which I cannot understand by means of the theories hitherto advanced, and this disposition is stronger than the change of the activity of the planets themselves through their own special powers. If there were only this aspect (Mars sextile Saturn), I would predict extreme cold owing to snowy exhalations, but, on account of the aggregation of several aspects, I think there will be such a disturbance, chiefly through the position of Mars) that the air will be heated by the warm vapors proceeding from the bowels of the Earth, that the snows will almost be melted, and the roads rendered impassable to a great extent. On the 4th of January, the conjunction of Sun-Mercury [indicates] snow and wind, according as the general disposition permits. By the 10th-11th [there will be] six very strong aspects, warmth, and rains intermixed with snows. Towards the end [of the month], none of the old aspects [will be in force], while of the new [aspects], by the 21st [there will be] the quintile of Jupiter and Venus—windy and warm, as much as winter permits. On the 28th, at the sesqui-square of Mars and the Sun, sharp [cold] is indicated, with light and stiff winds, and snow according to the conditions [prevailing]. Therefore, those who intend to investigate the new aspects, should direct their attention to these days.

Thesis 53

Many old and new aspects will occur in February. In the beginning [of the month] the Venus-Mercury conjunction will bring disturbances of the air, because, as seen before, and I speak here from experience, they have brought forth most of the contrariety of Saturn and Mars, which proves their configuration is exceedingly disturbing; perchance this is also due to the fact that they (Venus and Mercury), having nearly the same path, separate slowly and prove to be ponderous in some measure . To be sure, thunderstorms may also occur. From February 11th to 23rd there will be no calm (days). Thus, it will either snow a great deal, if the cold returns on the 11th with the square between Saturn and the Sun, or rain heavily, if, as I rather believe, warm weather continues.

Thesis 54

February had 21 aspects of six planets (there is almost no reason to include the lunar among the aspects as it is exceedingly speedy in movement. March has twenty (aspects), consequently the weather will be much more turbulent than heretofore, though this is contrary to its nature. During the first part of the month

21

(there will be) thunderstorms because of the Sun opposition Mars, and although much (force) is detracted (from the aspect) by the latitude of Mars, on the other hand, some power is added by the frequency of the aspects. Therefore, I predict a change from the hitherto unnatural heat into wintry cold on March 13th, (followed by) continuous cold wind and snow intermixed with rain.

Thesis 55

I expect a normal April, warm at the beginning, on account of the biquintile of Mars and the Sun, with rain about two days before and after the full moon, because all the planets are configurated [at this time]. Nor will the rains cease from the 13th to the 16th. Thereafter, [it will be] warm, and by the 24th, owing to the trine of the Sun and Mars, (there will be) an excess (of heat) which will break out in thunderstorms. Toward the end of the month, showers again.

The weather will be unpleasant and subject to thunderstorms during the first days of May due to the Venus-Mercury conjunction, unless the different latitude will weaken its [the aspect's] power, which is not quite certain, inasmuch as not even the days [are certain] because the calculation is still faulty. On the 10th, 11th and 12th, (there will be) cold rain and perhaps snow in mountainous regions, with the air unhealthy, yet when the sky is clear, one may also fear hoar-frost. Beautiful, mild, moist (weather) follows, for besides the old aspects, among the new is found the quintile of Saturn and Mars. Toward the end of the month, thunderstorms and showers will occur.

Thesis 56

I ought to write about the summer and also whether the year itself or the Earth will be in its proper (usual) state this year. But inasmuch as the universal cause of the disposition of the years is unknown, if the astrological conjectures about a particular year are erroneous because of such a great ignorance of the causes, I consider that they deserve forbearance. For they (the astrological conjectures) cannot be called useless, dealing as they do with a subject which is unquestionably of the greatest usefulness, if those conjectures which are hitherto hidden were brought out into the full light. And so I judge that the beginning of June will be hot and clear. After the full moon (there will be) dangerous disturbances, floods and frequent lightning. If the general disposition of the Earth should be inclined to dryness, there should be no danger. On the contrary, if it should be inclined to humidity, there will be no lightning, but continuous and cold rains. The end of the month is divided, as it were, in continuous stages according to its aspects. There will be commotions. I should think it likely that the following month will be slightly colder, owing to much moisture, unless for that matter, the whole year 1601 would be such. But if the year is universally inclined to dryness, the latter will be so much the greater during this month.

Thesis 57

Because it has 18 aspects, the augury for July is similar and of like uncertainty. For although there are about 150 aspects every year, this year the greater number of them accumulate (culminate) in the summer half year. The 1st, 2nd, 5th and 6th will be of moderate nature—windy, with showers. The 8th, rainy and cold; the 9th to 11th, breezy. The 12th, 13th and 14th are disturbed [influenced adversely] by the Venus-Mercury conjunction which is now repeated for the fourth time during this year, and violent storms may ensue. The 18th, 19th and 21st are of mixed nature, with impending thunder and rain storms. Thereafter, it will be clear and very hot, for by the beginning of August, Jupiter and Mars will be in conjunction.

Thesis 58

In August, at last (there will be) calm and heat. On the 5th, and likewise on the 9th, rain; and by the 15th, cold rains with thunderstorms. Following this, extreme heat and a great disturbance on the 19th.

Thesis 59

At the beginning of the month, September will be normal, rainy and foggy on the 11th and humid on the 15th and 17th. The 20th is very adversely influenced by the Saturn-Mars conjunction. If preceded by warm weather, there will now be terrible storms. If the year was generally humid, there will be heavy rains, with cold, and many fogs generally on these days. There will also be fog on the 27th. The other days will be normal.

Thesis 60

There will be cold rains on the 5th of October. Otherwise, the weather this month will be of the nature incurred by the preceding September. For as I have often stated, great importance attaches to the (particular) kind of terrestrial disposition found in any month. The 3rd, 9th and 27th will have violent rainstorms with roaring winds and rain on the 28th and 29th, but I consider that warmth will prevail, although the nature of some winds may be most cold, according to the region [of their origin].

Thesis 61

There will be the normal amount of hail storms in November, with stiff winds an the 5th. The 15th will be changeable and warm for this season of the year, due to the sextile of Jupiter and Venus. The 18th will have rain, but if clear, there will be the first frost, although it seems to me that cold is not yet probable, for the configuration of Jupiter, Mars and Venus toward the end of the month makes some days still warm and showery, with winds; these (aspects) will occasionally bring cold weather in some localities.

Thesis 62

The beginning of winter, December 3rd, will be a snowy and foggy day, though not very cold. From then onward, the aspects being quiescent, the weather will be clear, and as a result of this quiescence, only moderately cold. On the 15th, snow; no constant cold, but strong winds and pouring rains on the 19th. At Christmas time, there will be the sextile of Saturn and Mars which will increase the cold; after that the sextile of Venus and Mercury will cause more snow.

Thesis 63

I have omitted the configurations of the Moon with the other planets for the reason set forth above. However, for reasons also explained, one should not omit its ecliptic encounter with the Sun before the beginning of the year to come; nor the two ecliptic full moons (lunar eclipses) in opposite places of the sky, the one in 17° 48′ Gemini, whose beginning will be on the 9th of December at 7 minutes past 5 o'clock and the end at 33 minutes past 8 o'clock, according to an observation carried out here at Prague which comes very close to the calculation of Tycho; and the other, on the 4th of June, 1602 in 13° 32′ Sagittarius, whose beginning will be at 8 minutes to 5 o'clock p. m. below the Earth. It will begin in full darkness and end at 6 minutes past 9. But the beginning of the solar eclipse on the 24th of December, as I calculated it, is at 17 minutes past 1; the middle at 18 minutes to 3 o'clock in 2° 53′ Capricorn, ten inches from the Septentrion. The Sun sets before its end. This eclipse is very noticeable; therefore, if eclipses are capable of influencing anything, this (one) will have a great effect, especially in the Septentrion, where it also appears greatest. But I consider as unknown whether and in what way it will be effective in the year to come. For the rules of Ptolemy are uncertain and neither are they quite conformed to nature. In the year 1598 there was quite an extensive eclipse in Pisces; as the Sun came in the month of September to the antiscion-sign of Virgo, there were copious rains. In the year

1600, there was an eclipse in Cancer. As the sun returns into Gemini and Cancer, the weather will be wet both at that time and all the summer following. May the professors of these subjects consider whether the reasoning proceeds in a right manner, if I reject the forecast from this eclipse for December, 1602, and all that winter, and derive therefrom signs of great cold. Because if the eclipses obtain their power from the (particular) heavenly sign (admitting the influence of the eclipse, one has to admit also the influence of the sign), all three eclipses occur in aspects to Jupiter and Mars, wherefore they would portend adverse effects on natives of Jupiter, and warmth and harmful moistures, and thence impaired crops (natural products, etc.)

Thesis 64

On the 28th of November another Lunar eclipse will be seen by the occidentals, which, according to the calculation of Tycho, will begin here in Prague almost at the very moment when the Sun rises and the Moon sets. As this eclipse occurs below our horizon, as also does that Solar eclipse which will be seen on June 19th by the Occident, what use provoking tragic clamors about them? Surely those persons are ridiculous who consider it to be ominous that so many eclipses occur every year, as if four or five eclipses do not occur every year, if we consider all of the Earth's circumference. But these persons deceive themselves in that Origanus, in his recently published Ephemerides, computed many (eclipses) occurring all over the orb, which others were not wont to do before him.* And because of this (method of computation) it happened that those tragic vociferators never sensed these eclipses (which occurred) under our horizon. Staring in vain for new (things) in the sky, they wonder what there is new in Origanus' method.

Thesis 65

Predictions as to crops are very uncertain, for as regards natural things, everyone knows about divine Providence; the crop depends partly on fortuitous causes, and partly on the aforementioned general disposition of the year, of which factors the first by its very nature cannot be forecast and the second is still being

---

* David Origanus was born in Glatz, Bohemia, in 1558. His true family name, says Weidler, was Tost. He taught Greek and mathesis (mathematics or astrology) at the Academy in Francfort-on-the-Oder, where he also died in 1629. The ephemerides composed (compiled) by Origin (1595-1655) we mentioned l.c., and more will be said about them in the book, "De motibus Stallae Martis." At this place we will only note that the enumeration (listing) of the eclipses that are to occur in each year was given in the preface to the ephemerides (1599) in almost the same words as Kepler used in announcing his new attempt (undertaking).

sought. But the "parts"* used by astrologers for grain, grapes, wine, (olive) oil, wheat and so forth, and also the dispositions of Jupiter in a cardinal sign, are the vainest dreams. You ask why the wine-grapes did not grow well this year; it was because it has been a cold and wet year. Anyone who was able to foresee this would have been able to foresee the former (result) from this alone. You also ask why the rest of the crop was rich in one place and poor in another: it was because some regions of the Earth were humid, owing to some internal and hitherto undisclosed disposition of the Earth as above discussed, and the summer (weather) was satisfactorily clear; whereas elsewhere there was a dryness harmful to the fruits of the earth, which was also followed by an earthquake. Sometimes the year is good (productive) indeed, but suddenly and in one day, damage is caused by hoar-frost in mountainous regions and by floods in low lying parts, and this spreads over some one tract, whither the wind is directed. And great importance attaches to the nature of the winds, which are exceedingly inconstant in our regions. Thus, it is very stupid to seek causes for these events in the cardinal figures** while we see obvious causes before our eyes. And lest I seem to be an upstart confusing the art, I appeal to the authority of Cardan and Tycho.

Thesis 66

I shall consider one cause, weather, since there is no certainty as yet regarding the others. An early spring in southern parts causes a premature budding of the trees, and these still tender buds will be damaged by the arrival of an inclement March. In our climate there is usually nothing sprouting yet at that time on account of the usual cold and northern wind. The spring is favorable for the fruits of the earth, but there is danger on May 10th, 11th and 12th, as already has been stated. June menaces the flowering grape-vines, for at this time and during the following July, damages will result at different places either from excessive moisture or hail storms. August, September and October seem to favor the grapes as long as they remain on the branches, likewise the grain (crops). Nevertheless, there is danger around September 20th.

Thesis 67

As regards illnesses, the fact that a disturbance of the air will entail a disturbance of our bodies as well, is doubtless universally known to the physicians. Accordingly, if a variable

---

  * Ed. Note: Astrological rulerships.
  ** Equinox and solstice charts.

winter (in temperature) is prognosticated, there will also be many illnesses, particularly in the beginning of March and May. If, however, the summer also seems to be unsettled, the following autumn will be very bad as a result of the conjunction of Saturn and Mars, with many autumnal illnesses and the plague at some place where the noxious wind will carry it, especially if one takes into consideration the eclipses in the manner set forth. In general, any days I have noted previously as being affected adversely by abundant aspects will also produce illnesses in susceptible persons, and be harder for those already ill. If however, some person is already confined by illness, or if some bad (diseased) fluids are already circulating in the body, then of course, one should no longer disregard the configurations of the Moon with the other planets, particularly with the Sun, as I did heretofore. For they (the lunar aspects) particularly dispose and move the fluids (a fact which is evidenced by that huge chaos of fluids, the ocean), and I would not deny that it is useful to take this into consideration in practicing medicine. If possible, a doctor should use great caution with a weakened patient when the moon is situated in a strong aspect. For any aspect is a purgation of nature *per se*. And on the contrary, if strong purgations are needed, he should choose strong configurations. In fact, the whole matter of crises depends on the revolution of the Moon and (its) configuration with the (other) planets, and it is in vain that (the cause) is sought elsewhere.*

Thesis 68

If one grants the things I called above the foundation in regard to the harmony of the soul with the heavenly configurations, the astrologer has, in sooth, a say in political matters and in war. For with the strong aspects effective, any sort of minds are naturally active and cheerful at their work, and most of all, if the aspect is congenial with the considered individual as regards his horoscope. This sympathy, in the sence of the temperament of the body such as the heavens exert upon the air, does not act both upon the temperament of the body and upon the spirit; but, on the contrary, the spirit has sympathy *per se* to the heavens, because it has a resemblance (relationship) with the light and harmony, and afterwards it also transforms its body. Inasmuch as man is a sociable animal, minds unite in the greatest degree for public work (when) the rays of the planets associate geometrically in the heavens. However, the matter can be treated so much better

---

* Ed. Note—In connection with Kepler's statement that crises depend on the revolutions of the Moon, see the deductions of the modern statistician K. E. Kraft, page 38, June 1941 American Astrology.

if the nativity of those who (to use a Tychonian expression) govern the public fates, tend to harmonize.

Thesis 69

And it is certainly most foolish to look for particulars from this source* such as the curious seek to find in calendars (almanacs). For that which I stated in the Meteorology ought also to be held (true) here; from astrology one may demand nothing more than some excess of impulse of the soul; what (excess of impulse) there is going to be in a given case depends upon the freest exercise of will in political statesmen, who are made in the image of God, not (being) offsprings of nature and other causes. Accordingly, whether there shall be peace or war in some region shall be determined by those who are versed in political affairs and who possess the faculty of prediction in a measure no less than that of the astrologer. For politics too have their rules, so to speak, as well as the influence of the heavens. However, if there will be war in some region, then the souls (minds) of the soldiers and chiefs will be greatly prepared for stratagems, fights, battles, and other actions on the following days: Jan. 12th, Feb. 5th, 14th, 24th; March 5th, 14th; April 5th, 25th; May 4th, 12th, 31st; June 9th, 21st; July 8th, 13th, 19th; Aug. 1st, 9th, 15th, 25th, 30th; Sept. 20th, 27th; October 3rd; Nov. 5th, 18th, 30th; Dec. 25th. For this has been proven by experience.

Thesis 70

However, universal and perceptible or entirely new earthquakes seem not to be indicated by signs from the heavens in the fact that Saturn and Jupiter are not configurated (together) through the sky this year; but this is merely one and the most general cause and sign of great quakes. For in sublunar affairs there are in addition some other more particular and real things whose foresight does not rightfully concern the astrologer. Thus, consider that earthquake which last September in 1601 greatly shook the country all along the Rhine and the neighboring regions, for it is said that it was felt even in Insubria.** I state this not from astrology because an earthquake is not a thing pertaining to the stars, but from an examination of the world and of the seasons, from which it is to be seen that movements of armed men and minds usually follow earthquakes.

Thesis 71

There may be added mainly four (aspects) which have special significance; the eclipse of the Sun in 3° Capricorn; the

---

* Ed. Note— Daily aspects.

** A country in the neighborhood of Milan.

sextile of Saturn and the "stationary" Mars, which lasts almost throughout January and February and returns in the month of June; the conjunction of Jupiter and Mars at the end of July, and the conjunction of Saturn and Mars in the month of September. Firstly, it is proven by experience that under these two conjunctions, souls (spirits) are generally stunned, frightened or aroused in the expectation of revolts—which facts, when converging on a great multitude of men at one and the same place, have great importance either for achievement or for destruction, as war experience shows. The disaster of Erlau took place in the year 1596 when Jupiter and Mars were in opposition; the massacre of St. Bartholomew when Saturn and Mars were in conjunction, likewise in Scorpio, in the year 1572.*

In fact, I should consider it useful for the masters and rulers of the people to occupy themselves in this regard.** Because, for the ruling of the multitude (people), skill is necessary as well as a knowledge of things that commonly excite the minds. Thus, if at any place they prefer to keep peace and quiet, or if an insurrection may be feared, no meetings or assemblies should be held in August or September, and if any (are held), they should be dispersed and certainly, the causes exasperating the minds of the people should be speedily removed, or else the thought of the people should be changed by presenting something new. However, if some bold action is to be undertaken which is to be carried out by causing fear, it should be done in August; but if the mind is also to be hardened for work, let it be (done in) September. Yet if the enemy should dare to try anything during these months, one should prevent frightening the minds (of the people) by suitable remedies. For the fact that these remedies are also in our power and as it happens, events are not absolutely predestined, has been shown by a most clear example even during the last year.

Thesis 72

In the second place, faith (in) and esteem of a commander is a great strength to an army, for any victory depends on the driving force of the spirit. Yet if the commander is (held) in contempt on account of an affliction caused by his natal horoscope, this will contribute through imagination to the danger of the army

---

    * The city of Erlau was captured by the Turks in the year 1596. When the Archduke Maximilian wanted to recapture it, a great battle ensued. There were many people killed and his army had no success and retreated in disorder. The massacre of St. Bartholomew, the perfidious slaughter of the Huguenots at Paris, took place on the 17th of August, 1572.

    ** Ed. Note—To pay particular attention to the periods of culmination of these aspects.

as well as to the chances of war. Accordingly, as the Venus-Mars conjunction occurred in Poland at the rising (of the Sun), and the Solar eclipse was strongest in Muscovy (Russia) and Poland and and there is war there already, I think that these indications portend a defeat in the war. If someone (some commander) will transmute this stimulation through his nativity, he will inflict defeat; but if peace is strengthened in the meantime, there is absolutely no danger from the heavens alone.

Thesis 73

Thirdly, our fatherland is also affected by that conjunction already mentioned, for this is very spacious, not merely in the heavens, but certain sublunar causes have effect on some parts of it. For although the Sun shines on the universe and heats it, it (the Sun) still does not produce vegetables except where they are planted. And yet we expect, on account of an earthquake, and a "genesis" and a Solar eclipse that pertains to the place of the Sun in Wales and Spain, something particular in Sweden, Switzerland, Northern Italy and neighboring Gaul.

Thesis 74

I added the aforementioned sextile to the Jupiter-Mars conjunction because they have reference to the horoscopes of certain political persons. Thus, they will be operative this year, whether fortunately or unfortunately depends on the native's will (next to God). However, the hot planet, Mars, if it is not very strong, may affect nature as it moves along toward Virgo, and if, at the opposition to the Sun in March, it affects the nativity.

Thesis 75

I know that from a conjunction of Jupiter and Mars occurring in 17° Libra, the astrologers are wont to predict the death of some illustrious war leader, more particularly if any (planet) occupies a particular place (in Libra) in the horoscope. Lest this be turned into calumny, as if the heavens might be said to be turned to the destruction of men, it (such a prediction) should be explained differently. For the sense, in fact, is this: that just as this aspect is fiery *per se* and belongs to the famous planets, so likewise has experience proved it to be commonly found in illustrious families. Yet as almost any commotion (stimulation) of the body or spirit, or a transition to a new state, takes place when the heavens correspond to a horoscope* it happens that some illustrious persons act under these aspects or similar (ones);

---

* Ed. Note: When the transiting planetary pattern repeats aspects in the natal chart.

30

for in such a multitude, some (persons) are indeed born under such (aspects). But that stimulation, while it brings destruction to ill-disposed subjects, also elevates the stronger to great things by reason of age or gallantry; either of these conditions may take place in different persons this year, but neither are absolutely necessary.

Conclusion

I had, in view of these theses which I thought to state and defend on physical grounds in regard to the fundamentals of astrology and the coming year 1602. If the professors of physics (natural history) consider them deserving of their consideration and communicate their objections to me for the sake of establishing the truth, if God gives (me) ability, I shall reply in the prognostic for the following year. To this controversy I invite all persons who are philosophizing in earnest. For it concerns the honor (glory) of God, the creator, and the usefulness for the human race.

Meanwhile I pray for a most happy New Year for all and each of you through Christ, the Mediator.